Sharon
Thompson

RECIPES FROM A KENTUCKY
BLACKBERRY PATCH

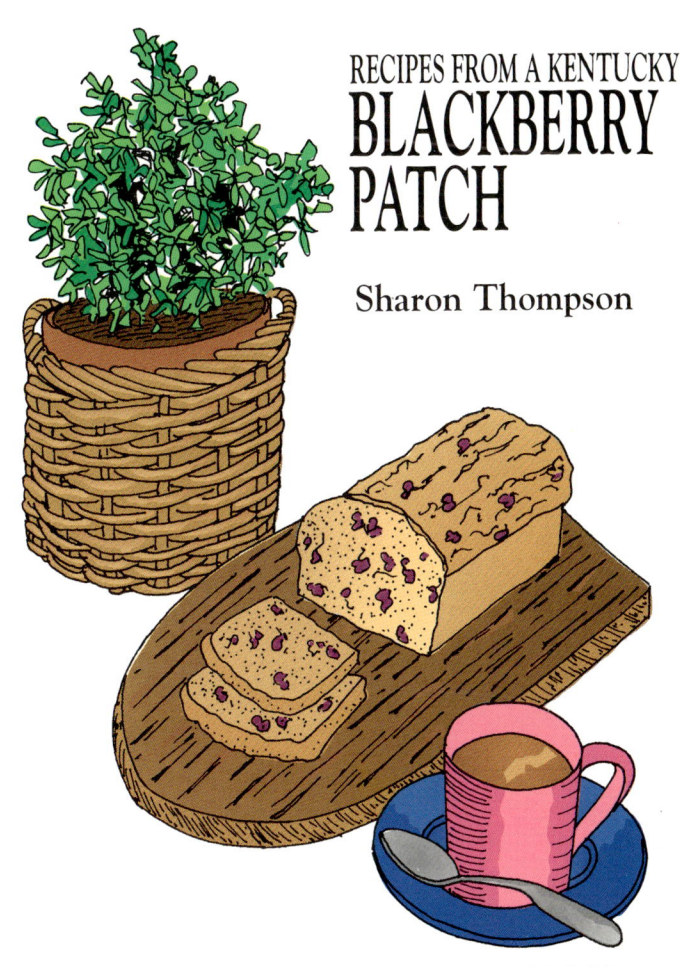

Sharon Thompson

ILLUSTRATED BY SUSAN BRUBAKER

WindStone Farms

Published in 1993

RECIPES FROM A KENTUCKY
BLACKBERRY PATCH
© 1993 by WindStone Farms

All rights reserved. Printed in the U.S.
No part of this book may be reproduced in any form, by photostat, microfilm, xerography or any other means, or incorporated into any information retrieval system, electronic or mechanical, without the written permission of the copyright owner.

All inquiries should be addressed to:
WindStone Farms
3948 Pleasant Springs Road
Carlisle, Kentucky 40311

LIBRARY OF CONGRESS CATALOG CARD NUMBER:
92-82075

INTERNATIONAL STANDARD BOOK NUMBER:
0-9635603-0-1

INTRODUCTION

This cookbook was written out of love for the blackberry.

Picking berries on a hot summer day and coming home with chigger bites are fond memories for a lot of country people.

Wayne and Kay Shumate, owners of WindStone Farms in Carlisle, Kentucky, have several acres of their farmland planted in blackberries. Wayne, a successful businessman, spends his free time growing blackberries and thinking of new ways to use them. The blackberry crop is a small business that developed because of his now pleasant childhood memories of fighting the cantankerous blackberry brier.

Kay, who manages the day-to-day picking and tending of the blackberries, has sweet childhood memories that sour only at harvest time. "In July — when we're picking them, it's so hot and our clothes are stained and we're tired — I never want to see another blackberry." But she loves being in the patch and watching the berries grow. Kay remembers picking blackberries as a child and especially going home with unpleasant chigger bites. It was fun for Kay because she lived in the city and was fascinated with the country. "It didn't seem like a chore for me," she said.

Sharon Thompson and the Shumates have compiled some of their favorite blackberry recipes in this book. Sharon is food writer for the *Lexington Herald-Leader*, the major newspaper in Central Kentucky. She has 20 years of food writing experience and fond memories as well.

Everyone who has picked wild blackberries can recite a funny story or two about fighting bees and avoiding snakes in the brambles.

We hope this little book brings back wonderful memories for you, or, introduces you to the most beautiful of all berries.

Nasty brier patch grows friendlier with age

I once hated blackberries.

My father, Claude Wiseman, has picked wild blackberries for 25 years in a patch across the road from where he lives. Each summer he would say, "Oh, those berries are the biggest I've ever seen. Come pick with me." And for the last 25 years I've been big enough to say no.

But before that time, I was forced into picking blackberries.

When I was a child, my family lived in rural Clark County, Kentucky, and every summer we picked blackberries. We walked what seemed like miles from our house, down the railroad track, to a valley and then up the hillside to the brier patch.

I still remember putting on old baggy pants and long-sleeve shirts (so the briers wouldn't scratch my arms) and hanging a bucket on my belt.

Off we'd go to the patch — my mother, my two brothers and several neighbors. It was an event. We packed lunch and took ice water in a Mason jar.

And no one was allowed to go home until all the huge water buckets were filled with juicy blackberries.

Those days were the worst I can remember. It was hot. June bugs and yellow and black garden spiders were everywhere. I would cry. I came home with chigger bites. I hated blackberries. I hated jam.

When I was 12 we left Clark County and that dreadful blackberry patch, and I vowed never to touch another blackberry.

One day when I was in my mid-thirties, my father said to me, "I went blackberry picking today. Those are the biggest blackberries I've ever seen." They must be gigantic, I thought, given that they've been growing bigger each year for 25 years.

I had to see for myself. I decided to walk over to the patch and see what the berries looked like. It would be wonderful to have fresh jam to give friends at Christmastime.

So off I went, with the bucket tied around my waist. I picked a few berries around the edges of the patch and the more I picked the more I enjoyed it. A brier snagged my arm, but I kept going deeper and deeper in the patch.

In just a matter of minutes, my bucket was filled with beautiful blackberries.

My feelings about berries and briers have definitely changed. I was very delighted with the bucket of berries I picked. With berry-stained hands and clothes and muddy shoes, I ran to a grocery store to buy canning jars, sugar and Sure-Jell.

As I capped those lovely jars of jam, I was very proud of having "discovered" something as wonderfully fresh and delicious as the blackberry.

The next evening, I said to my 8-year-old daughter: "Come pick blackberries with me. They're the biggest I've ever seen."

I put a baggy shirt and pants on her and tied a bucket around her tiny waist. And off we went to the blackberry patch.

But somehow, buzzing June bugs, prickly bushes and blackberry juice on her hands did not appeal to her.

I smiled and took her home.

—*By Sharon Thompson*
Reprinted with permission of the *Lexington Herald-Leader*

Aunt Gin's Jam Cake

2 cups self-rising flour
½ teaspoon nutmeg
3 teaspoons cinnamon
3 tablespoons cocoa
1 cup chopped nuts
2 cups sugar
½ cup oil
3 eggs
1 cup buttermilk
1 ½ cups blackberry jam
3 tablespoons evaporated milk

Grease tube pan and line bottom with waxed paper. Mix dry ingredients and set aside.

Cream oil and sugar, then add eggs and beat well. Stir in buttermilk and add dry ingredients, mixing well. Add jam and evaporated milk. Pour into tube pan. Bake at 350 degrees one hour, or until a toothpick inserted comes out clean. Top with caramel icing.

To make caramel icing: Pour 1 ½ cups confectioners' sugar into metal mixing bowl and set aside. Mix 1 ½ cups brown sugar, ¼ stick butter and ⅓ cup milk in saucepan. Boil 1 ½ minutes. While still hot, pour over confectioners' sugar and beat with mixer until smooth and thick enough to spread.

Bourbon Jam Cake

1 cup butter
1 ½ cups sugar
4 egg yolks
4 cups all-purpose flour
½ teaspoon cloves
½ teaspoon nutmeg
1 teaspoon cinnamon
Pinch salt
1 teaspoon soda (dissolved in warm water)
1 cup buttermilk
1 cup black walnuts
2 cups blackberry jam
4 egg whites, beaten until stiff
Kentucky bourbon

Cream butter and sugar together. Add egg yolks one at a time, beating well after each addition. Sift flour before measuring (reserve ¼ cup flour to dredge nuts).

Add spices and salt to flour and sift. Add dissolved soda to buttermilk. Gradually add in flour mixture, alternately with buttermilk, to the butter, sugar and egg mixture. Beat after each addition.

Dredge nuts in reserved flour. Stir in nuts and blackberry jam. Fold in beaten egg whites. Pour into greased and floured tube pan. Bake at 350 degrees for 40 to 50 minutes. Remove from pan and drizzle warm cake with Kentucky bourbon. Frost with caramel icing.

Margaret's Blackberry Cobbler

2 cups fresh blackberries, washed and picked over
1 cup flour
½ cup sugar
1 teaspoon baking powder
1 stick butter, melted
½ cup milk
½ teaspoon vanilla
1 cup sugar
½ cup hot water

Place blackberries in the bottom of a 9- by 9-inch square pan. Combine flour, ½ cup sugar, baking powder, melted butter, milk and vanilla. Pour over fruit. Combine 1 cup sugar and water and pour over batter. Bake in 350-degree oven for about 45 minutes. Frozen blackberries may be used.

Summer is the only time you'll find fresh blackberries at the supermarket. They are very fragile and don't travel well at all. If you're blessed with living close to a patch, pick as many as possible to freeze or can. And eat as many as your stomach will hold.

Blackberry Mountain Pie

1 stick margarine
1 cup self-rising flour
1 cup sugar
1/2 cup milk
3 cups fresh blackberries, washed and picked over
2 1/2 cups water
1 3/4 cups sugar

Melt margarine in 9- by 13-inch baking dish. Set aside. Mix flour, 1 cup sugar and milk. Beat until smooth and creamy. Pour batter into baking dish with melted butter.

Combine blackberries, water and 1 3/4 cups sugar. Stir until sugar dissolves. Pour over batter. Do not stir. Bake at 350 degrees, about 25 minutes, or until golden brown.

When buying fresh blackberries, make sure the berries were mature and ripe when harvested. The tiny seed-bearing spheres that make up each berry are called drupelets. Green, pale or off-color drupelets are a sign of immaturity.

Grilled Chicken Salad with Blackberries

6 boneless, skinless chicken breasts
1 head red leaf lettuce
1 small head Boston lettuce
1 bunch of radishes, quartered
4 green onions, cut lengthwise and into thirds
2 cups fresh blackberries, rinsed

Marinade:
1/2 cup soy sauce
1/2 cup water
2 tablespoons lemon juice
1 tablespoon brown sugar
2 tablespoons oil
1/4 teaspoon hot pepper sauce
1 clove garlic, minced
1/4 teaspoon pepper

Dressing:
1/2 cup sugar
1/2 cup vinegar
1 clove garlic
Salt to taste
Freshly ground black pepper
1 cup vegetable oil

To make marinade: Combine all marinade ingredients and store in airtight container in refrigerator.

To make dressing: Put sugar, vinegar, garlic, salt and pepper in food processor or blender. Slowly add oil and puree until smooth.

Place chicken breasts in marinade and let stand for 20 minutes. Grill until done. Chill and slice into strips. Lay a bed of lettuce on six plates. Top with chicken strips. Sprinkle cut green onions and quartered radishes over salad. Drizzle with dressing and arrange blackberries on plate. Serves 6.

Blackberry Mousse

½ cup cold milk
1 envelope unflavored gelatin
1 cup milk, heated to boiling
1 ½ cups frozen blackberries, thawed
¼ cup sugar
2 cups frozen whipped topping, thawed

Pour cold milk into blender. Sprinkle unflavored gelatin over milk; let stand 2 minutes. Add hot milk and process at low speed until gelatin is completely dissolved, about 2 minutes. Add blackberries and sugar; process until blended, about 1 minute. Pour into large bowl and with wire whisk blend in whipped topping. Pour into a trifle bowl or individual dessert cups. Chill until firm, about 3 hours. Serves 6.

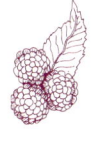

Avoid overripe berries. They look dull and mushy. Mold on the fruit is evidence that it has been stored too long.

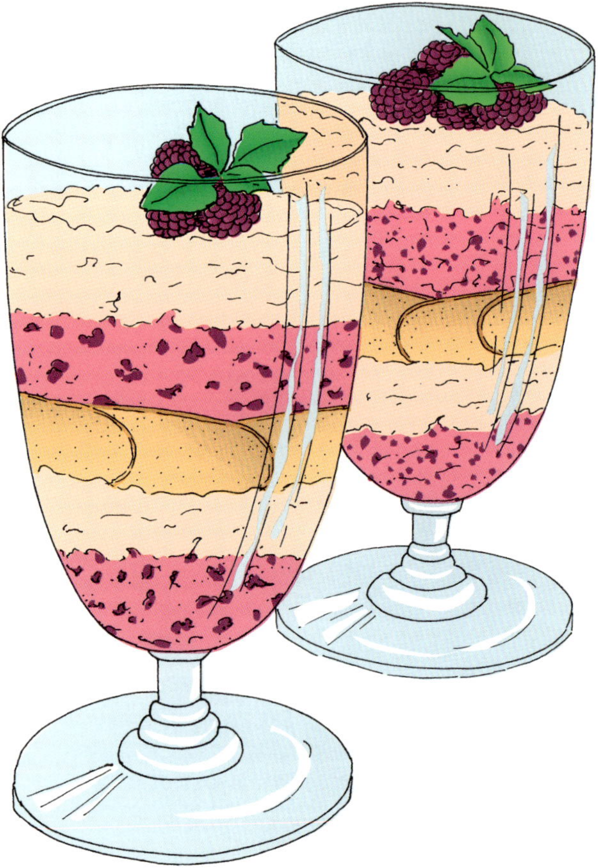

Triple Layer Pudding

2 cups fresh blackberries, washed and picked over
¾ cup sugar, divided
2 cups heavy cream
6 ladyfingers

Toss the berries with ½ cup sugar and set aside for 1 hour. Berries will give off juice. Whip cream until stiff peaks form with remaining ¼ cup of sugar. Cover and refrigerate. Cut the ladyfingers into 1-inch squares.

In four goblets, place several berries along with 1 tablespoon of juice per serving. Spread 2 tablespoons whipped cream on top of the berries.

Cover the whipped cream with a layer of ladyfinger pieces. Repeat the procedure, layering berries with juice, whipped cream and ladyfinger pieces until each goblet is filled. Cover and refrigerate overnight. Top with remaining whipped cream and a few berries as garnish.

Serves 4.

Leaky berries are either overripe or damaged. Staining on the carton means the berries have been leaking juices.

Blackberry Swirl Cheesecake

2 8-ounce packages cream cheese, softened
½ cup sugar
½ teaspoon vanilla
2 eggs
1 9-inch ready-to-use graham cracker crust
3 tablespoons seedless blackberry jam

Mix cream cheese, sugar and vanilla at medium speed with electric mixer until well blended. Add eggs and mix until blended.

Pour into crust. Dot top of cheesecake with jam. Cut through batter with knife several times for marble effect. Bake at 350 degrees for 40 minutes or until center is almost set. Cool. Refrigerate 3 hours or overnight. Makes 8 servings.

Soft berries also freeze very well covered in a 40 percent syrup (4 cups water plus 3 cups sugar). Pack them in rigid, airtight containers and leave ½-inch head space. This is the best method if you want to serve the thawed berries without cooking. They will keep for 10 to 12 months at zero degrees.

Blackberry Vinegar

1 cup fresh blackberries, washed and picked over
1 cup white vinegar

Heat vinegar. Place fruit in a jar and cover with warm vinegar. When cool, screw lid on jar. Store in a cool, dark place for 7 to 10 days. Taste. If the flavor of the fruit is prominent, it's ready. If the flavor is weak, set it aside for a few more days. You can leave the berries in or strain them out through a piece of cheesecloth. Store in a dark, cool place.

Blackberries must be ripened on the bush and picked when they are already soft, then rushed to the kitchen before they spoil.

Blackberry Bundt Cake

1 package pound cake mix
2 cups fresh blackberries, washed and picked over
1 ½ tablespoons flour
¼ cup dark brown sugar

Prepare cake according to package directions. Toss the blackberries with the flour to coat lightly, then toss them with the brown sugar. Pour ⅓ of the cake batter into the Bundt pan, distribute ½ of the berries on top, add another layer of batter, another layer of blackberries and finish with the last of the batter. Bake in a preheated 350-degree oven for 1 hour. Let rest 15 minutes before turning out. Sprinkle cake with powdered sugar. Makes 1 Bundt cake.

If you don't like the seeds that are in blackberries, get rid of them. Here's how.

Blackberry Puree

Put 1 quart perfectly fresh blackberries, washed and picked over, and 1 ½ cups sugar in the bowl of a food processor. Process until blackberries are reduced to a fine pulp. Do not overprocess or it will become juice and the seeds will be pulverized. Press through a sieve just fine enough to contain the seeds. Makes 4 ½ cups.

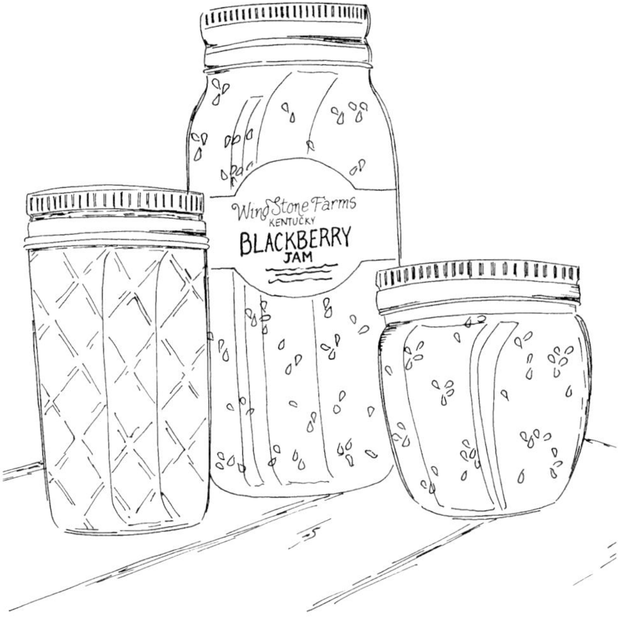
WindStone Farms
KENTUCKY
BLACKBERRY
JAM

Berried Treasure

1 9-inch pie crust, baked
1 ½ cups fresh blackberries, washed and picked over
4 egg whites
⅛ teaspoon salt
1 cup sugar

Put egg whites in mixing bowl. Add salt and beat very stiff. Slowly add half of the sugar, beating constantly. Beat another 3 minutes until egg whites are very stiff. Gradually add the remaining sugar, using a spoon. Fold in berries. Pile the berry mixture into the cooled pie shell. Sprinkle a few fresh blackberries over the top and sprinkle 1 or 2 tablespoons of sugar over all. Place in a 325-degree oven for 15 to 20 minutes until meringue is done and is a golden brown. Makes one 9-inch pie.

Buy blackberries that are bright, clean and dry. Berries should be plump and deeply colored. Berries really should look picture perfect.

Blackberry Cheese Fluff

1 pound fresh blackberries, washed and picked over
½ cup sugar
1 tablespoon rum
¼ teaspoon ground cinnamon
2 envelopes unflavored gelatin
1 cup yogurt cheese (see note)
5 egg whites

Press the blackberries through a fine sieve or food mill to puree and remove the seeds. You should have about 1¼ cups of puree. Place 1 cup of the puree, sugar, rum and cinnamon in a saucepan over low heat and cook, stirring, until the sugar is dissolved, about 10 minutes.

Sprinkle the gelatin over the remaining ¼ cup puree and let stand 1 minute. Stir the gelatin into the hot mixture and stir to dissolve completely. Place in the refrigerator to cool for 30 minutes.

Beat the yogurt cheese into the cooled berry mixture. Beat the egg whites until soft peaks form and fold them into the berry mixture. Spoon mixture into a 1½-quart decorative bowl. Refrigerate at least 6 hours before serving. Makes 6 servings.

To make yogurt cheese: Pour 16-ounce container of plain low-fat yogurt into a cheesecloth-lined colander. The cheesecloth should be of very fine weave. Tie the four corners of the cheesecloth. Cover with plastic wrap and place in refrigerator and let drain 12 to 24 hours or until the yogurt has stopped draining.

Blackberry Cheesecake Bars

Base:
1 cup all-purpose flour
3 tablespoons confectioners' sugar
7 tablespoons unsalted butter, cut into 7 pieces, at room temperature
½ teaspoon vanilla extract
1 egg white for glazing

Topping:
½ cup fresh or frozen blackberries
8 ounces cream cheese, at room temperature
1 cup sour cream
7 tablespoons granulated sugar
2 large egg yolks
1 teaspoon vanilla extract
2 teaspoons all-purpose flour

Preheat oven to 350 degrees. Lightly grease an 8-inch square baking pan.

To make base: Process the flour and confectioners' sugar in a food processor for several seconds. Add the butter and vanilla and process until the dough comes together, 20 to 30 seconds.

Pat the dough gently over the bottom of the prepared pan about 1½ inches up the sides. Glaze it with the egg white. Pour the egg white on the dough and tip the pan from side to side so that the white spreads over the surface. Pour off excess.

Bake the base on the center oven rack until lightly golden, about 30 minutes. Place the base in the refrigerator for 15 minutes to cool completely. Keep the oven on.

To make topping: Wrap the blackberries in paper towels to absorb any liquid. Place the remaining topping ingredients in a food processor and process until blended, about 15 seconds.

Pour the topping evenly over the base, then arrange the blackberries evenly on the topping. Place the bars on the center oven rack until set, about 1 hour. Allow them to cool completely, then refrigerate overnight.

The next day cut the bars with a sharp knife that is dipped in hot water and wiped dry before each cut. Allow the bars to warm to room temperature before serving. Makes 12 bars.

The blackberry is a nourishing and refreshing fruit, containing 85 percent water and 10 percent carbohydrates. It is a good source of vitamin B$_1$ and mineral salts, especially calcium.

Berry Cream Coffee Cake

2 1/4 cups all-purpose flour
3/4 cup sugar
3/4 cup margarine, softened
1 cup yogurt cheese or 8-ounce carton light sour cream
1 egg
1/2 teaspoon baking powder
1/2 teaspoon baking soda

1/4 teaspoon salt
1 teaspoon vanilla extract
1/4 cup sugar
1 8-ounce package cream cheese, softened
1 egg
1/2 cup blackberry jam
1/2 cup sliced almonds

Heat oven to 350 degrees. In a large mixer bowl stir together flour and 3/4 cup sugar. Cut in margarine until crumbly. Reserve 1 cup crumb mixture for topping. Add light sour cream, egg, baking powder, baking soda, salt and vanilla to remaining crumb mixture. Beat at medium speed, scraping bowl often, until well mixed (1 to 2 minutes). Spread batter over bottom and 2 inches up sides of greased and floured 9-inch springform pan.

In small mixer bowl combine 1/4 cup sugar, cream cheese and egg. Beat at medium speed, scraping bowl often, until smooth (1 to 2 minutes). Spread cream cheese mixture over batter within 1/2 inch from edge. Spread jam over cream cheese mixture. Sprinkle almonds and 1 cup reserved crumb mixture over jam. Bake for 45 to 60 minutes or until cream cheese filling is set and crust is dark golden brown.

Cool 15 minutes; remove from pan. Serve warm or cold. Refrigerate. Makes 16 servings.

Berry Good Cheesecake Bars

¾ cup butter or margarine
⅓ cup firmly packed brown sugar
1 ¼ cups all-purpose flour
1 cup oats, uncooked
½ cup seedless blackberry jam
2 8-ounce packages cream cheese, softened
¾ cup sugar
2 tablespoons all-purpose flour
2 eggs
3 tablespoons lemon juice

Heat oven to 350 degrees. Spray a 13- by 9- by 2-inch pan with cooking spray.

To make crust: Combine butter and brown sugar. Beat at medium speed of electric mixer until well blended. Add 1¼ cups flour and oats gradually at low speed. Mix until well blended. Press into bottom of greased pan. Bake at 350 degrees for 20 minutes.

To make filling: Spoon jam immediately on hot crust. Spread carefully to cover. Combine cream cheese, sugar and 2 tablespoons flour in large bowl. Beat at low speed until well blended. Add eggs. Mix well. Add lemon juice. Beat until smooth. Pour over blackberry layer. Bake at 350 degrees for 25 minutes or until set. Cool at room temperature. Cut into bars about 2- by 1 ½-inches. Cover. Refrigerate. Makes 3 dozen bars.

Black and Blue Salad

2 3-ounce packages blackberry gelatin
2 cups boiling water
1 20-ounce can crushed pineapple, undrained
1 can blueberry pie filling
½ cup chopped nuts

Topping:
8 ounces cream cheese, softened
8 ounces sour cream
1 teaspoon vanilla
½ cup sugar

Dissolve gelatin in boiling water. Add crushed pineapple, pie filling and chopped nuts. Pour into 9- by 13-inch baking dish. Chill until set.
   To make topping: Combine cream cheese and sour cream. Add vanilla and sugar. Mix well and spread on top of gelatin mixture. Makes 10 to 12 servings.

Cultivation of the blackberry began around 1825.

Blackberry Dumplings

2 ¼ cups biscuit mix
⅔ cup milk
Additional biscuit mix
6 cups fresh blackberries, washed and picked over
1 ½ to 2 cups sugar
1 cup water

Prepare dumpling dough by combining biscuit mix with milk to form a soft dough. Beat for 30 seconds. Sprinkle work surface with additional biscuit mix. Turn dough onto work surface and roll dough into a ball. Knead lightly 10 times, keeping work surface dusted with biscuit mix. Roll or pat dough lightly to ½-inch thickness and cut with a 2-inch biscuit cutter dipped in baking mix. Set rolled dumplings aside.

In a large pot, mix blackberries with sugar and water. Measurements for the syrup needn't be exact, but to taste. Bring to a slow boil, being careful not to scorch the fruit. Cook for about 5 minutes. Adjust the syrup to a very low boil or simmer.

Place dumplings around the surface of the fruit mixture. Cover pot and cook gently for 10 minutes. Uncover pot and let cook for 10 minutes more. Remove from heat and let mixture cool in pot for up to 1 hour.

Serve by spooning a dumpling into each individual serving dish. Spoon the fruit filling with syrup over top. Makes up to 12 servings.

Blackberry Tea Bread

1 cup butter
1 ½ cups sugar
1 teaspoon vanilla
¼ teaspoon lemon extract
4 eggs
3 cups all-purpose flour
1 teaspoon salt
1 teaspoon cream of tartar
½ teaspoon baking soda
1 cup blackberry jam
½ cup low-fat yogurt
1 cup chopped pecans

Heat oven to 350 degrees. Cream butter, sugar, vanilla and lemon extract until fluffy. Add eggs, one at a time, beating well after each addition.

Stir together flour, salt, cream of tartar and soda. Combine jam and yogurt. Add jam mixture and dry mixture alternately to butter mixture. Beat well until combined. Stir in nuts.

Spray a 9- by 5- by 3-inch loaf pan with cooking spray. Pour batter into prepared pan and bake in preheated oven for 55 minutes. Cool 20 minutes in pan. Remove from pan and cool completely on wire racks.

Triple Berry Refresher

1 12-ounce can undiluted evaporated milk
1 6- or 8-ounce container berry-flavored low-fat yogurt
½ cup fresh blueberries
½ cup fresh raspberries
½ cup fresh blackberries
2 tablespoons honey or to taste

In blender container, combine evaporated milk, yogurt, blueberries, raspberries, blackberries and honey. Cover and blend until smooth. If desired, strain to remove larger seeds. Serve over ice.

Makes 4 servings.

Many people think of the blackberry as an ingredient for desserts only, but it has a wine-like flavor that complements veal, roasted or grilled duck and squab. To make a sauce, crush the berries and add a splash of red wine to boost the acid balance if necessary. Strain the seeds from the sauce, adding fresh berries at the last second just to warm before serving.

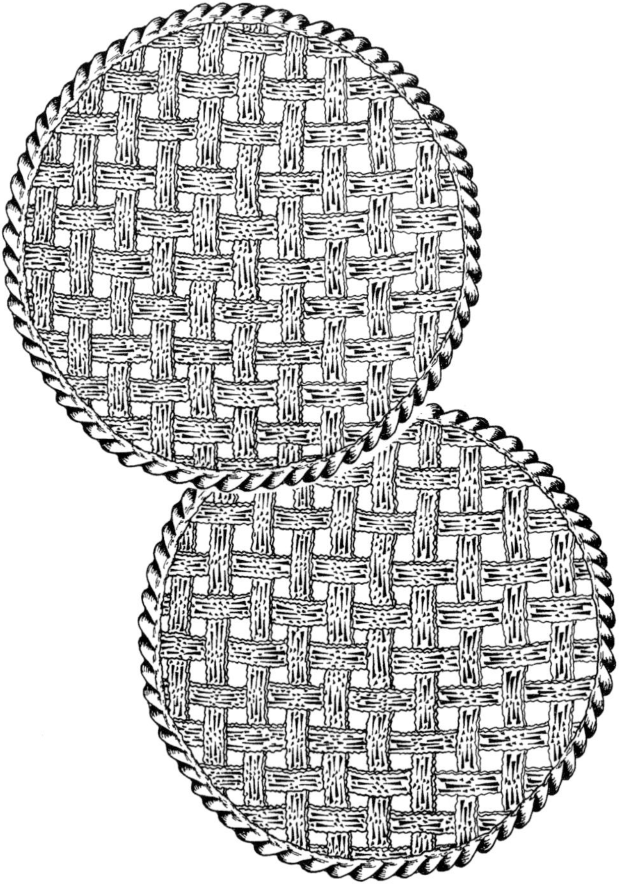

Blackberry Pie

Pastry for 1 double-crust 9-inch pie
1 cup sugar
3 tablespoons quick-cooking tapioca
¼ teaspoon salt
6 cups fresh blackberries, washed and picked over
2 tablespoons butter or margarine

Combine the sugar, tapioca and salt in a medium saucepan, stirring well to remove lumps. Add 3 cups of the berries and mix well. Cook over very low heat, stirring constantly, until mixture just starts to bubble.

Add butter and mix well. Remove from heat, stir in remaining berries and let cool.

Fit pastry into the pie plate, pour the cooled berry mixture into the shell and add a vented top crust (a lattice crust works particularly well; cut the pastry into ¾-inch strips and weave over filling. Seal edges). Bake 20 minutes at 400 degrees, then reduce heat to 350 and bake an additional 30 minutes, or until crust is golden brown.

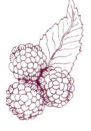

Blackberries freeze easily and are quite appealing, even though they are not as delectable as fresh.

Grandma's Blackberry Cobbler

5 cups fresh blackberries, washed and picked over
1 cup sugar
3 tablespoons all-purpose flour
2 tablespoons butter

Crust:
2 cups all-purpose flour
2 tablespoons sugar
4 teaspoons baking powder
½ teaspoon salt
¼ teaspoon cream of tartar
½ cup butter
½ cup milk

For filling, mix 1 cup sugar and flour, toss with blackberries and pour into buttered 1½-quart oblong dish. Dot with butter, set aside. To make crust, sift flour, sugar, baking powder, salt and cream of tartar. Mix in ½ cup butter until mixture resembles coarse meal. Mix in milk, and stir until it forms a ball of dough. Roll dough out ¼-inch thick on a floured board.

Cover blackberries with the dough and trim edges. Cut a vent in the center of the dough, and sprinkle the top generously with sugar.

Bake in a 400-degree oven for 40 minutes or until crust is golden. Serve whipped cream. You may substitute 1 quart canned blackberries.

Luscious Blackberry Custard

½ cup sugar, divided
2 egg yolks
2 cups heavy cream
½ cup fresh blackberries, washed and picked over

Heat oven to 350 degrees. Spray 4 6-ounce custard cups with non-stick cooking spray. Coat with 2 tablespoons sugar. Combine egg yolks with 4 tablespoons sugar. Blend until mixture is light yellow. Add heavy cream. Skim off surface foam. Add blackberries.

Add remaining 2 tablespoons sugar and a few drops of water. Set aside. Pour egg mixture into custard cups. Place cups in a 2-inch deep pan filled with enough water to reach halfway up sides of the cups.

Bake 45 minutes or until firm. Remove from pan and let cool, about an hour. Turn upside down on a dessert plate. Makes 4 servings.

The blackberry is a shrub commonly found along hedges, in woods and in untilled fields of most of the Northern Hemisphere, and also in South Africa. Its scientific name is *Rubus fruticosus*.

Blackberry Sherbet

1 pint fresh blackberries, washed and picked over
½ cup honey
½ cup evaporated milk
2 tablespoons lemon juice

Place all ingredients in a blender and process until smooth. Pour into ice cream freezer and freeze according to manufacturer's directions. Makes 2 pints.

To store blackberries: Sort through the berries and discard any crushed or moldy ones. Because they crush so easily blackberries should be stored in a single layer rather than dumped together in a carton. Keep the berries uncovered on the refrigerator shelf — not in a vegetable drawer — and they should last one to two days. Do not wash them until ready to eat.

Simple Jam Cake

1 frozen pound cake, thawed
¾ cup seedless blackberry jam
Powdered sugar

Slice pound cake in half lengthwise. Spread bottom layer with jam. Place other half on top. Dust the top with powdered sugar. Cut into 8 slices. Serves 8.

If you plan to use blackberries for cooking, simply spread washed berries on a tray and freeze them individually. Pack the frozen fruit in sealed plastic bags. You can then take out berries as you need them and reseal the bag.

Blackberry Dump Cake

1 package yellow cake mix
1 24-ounce jar blackberry cobbler filling
1 cup chopped pecans
1 stick butter or margarine, cut in thin slices

Heat oven to 350 degrees. Spray 13- by 9- by 2-inch pan with non-stick cooking spray. Dump blackberry cobbler filling into pan and spread evenly. Dump dry cake mix onto blackberry layer; spread evenly. Sprinkle pecans over cake mix. Put butter over top. Bake at 350 degrees for 45 minutes. Serve warm or cold. Makes 12 servings.

The blackberry was eaten by the first inhabitants of the planet, according to paleontological findings. Historical evidence is provided by Aeschylus and Hippocrates, 400 to 500 B.C.

Rolling Blackberry Cake

1 package angel food cake mix
¼ cup confectioners' sugar
1 24-ounce jar blackberry cobbler filling

Heat oven to 350 degrees. Line 15 ½- by 10 ½- by 1-inch jelly-roll pan with foil, allowing foil to extend about 1 inch above rim of pan.

Prepare cake according to package directions. Pour batter into lined pan and spread evenly. Cut through batter with knife or spatula to remove large air bubbles.

Bake for 25 to 30 minutes or until top springs back when lightly touched with fingertip. Immediately turn cake out onto a towel covered with confectioners' sugar. Gently peel off foil, then roll up with towel as for jelly roll. Cool.

Unroll cake and spread with blackberry cobbler filling to within 1 inch of edges; reroll. Trim ends. With small fine sieve, sift confectioners' sugar over roll. Makes 12 servings.

Blackberry Cake

2 cups sugar
2 sticks margarine
3 eggs
3 cups flour
1 teaspoon cocoa
½ teaspoon salt
1 teaspoon cinnamon
1 teaspoon allspice
2 teaspoons soda
2 cups fresh blackberries, juice and all
1 cup raisins
1 cup nuts

Cream sugar and margarine. Add eggs. Mix dry ingredients together. Add blackberries and juice, alternating with dry ingredients.

    Beat until smooth. Add raisins and nuts, which have been sprinkled with flour. Pour into greased and floured tube pan, and bake at 350 degrees 1½ hours or until done.

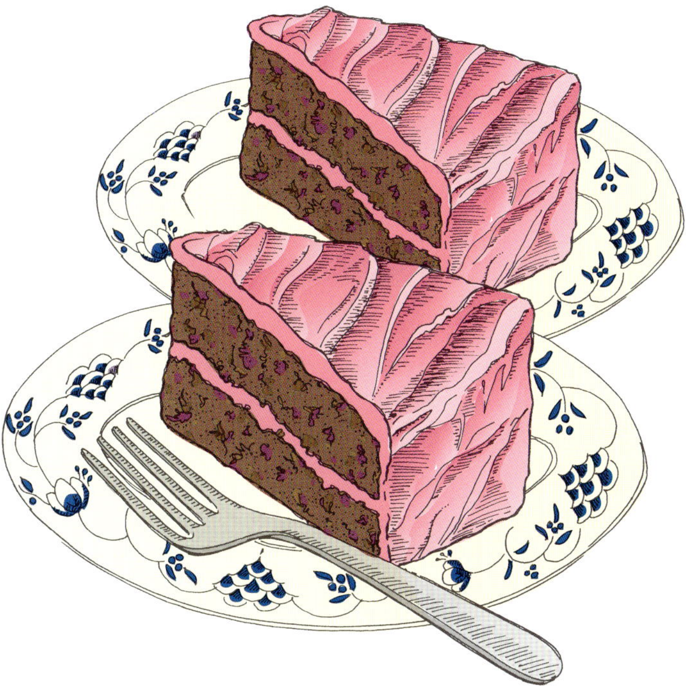

Blackberry Crunch Cake

1 24-ounce jar blackberry cobbler filling
1 package yellow cake mix
1 cup packed brown sugar
1 stick butter or margarine, melted

Heat oven to 350 degrees. Spread cobbler filling in bottom of ungreased 9- by 9- by 2-inch square pan. Combine dry cake mix, brown sugar and melted butter. Mixture will be crumbly. Sprinkle over cobbler filling. Bake for 45 minutes or until golden brown. Makes 10 servings.

The dewberry and blackberry look exactly alike. The dewberry is a trailing, ground-running berry. The blackberry grows on an erect plant.

Hidden Berry Cake

1 package yellow cake mix
1 14-ounce can sweetened condensed milk
3 tablespoons lemon juice
1 cup fresh blackberries, washed and picked over

Heat oven to 375 degrees. Spray two 8½- or 9- by 1½-inch round layer pans with cooking spray. Prepare, bake and cool cake as directed on package.

For filling, put sweetened condensed milk and lemon juice into medium bowl; stir until well blended. Mix in blackberries. Spread between cooled layers. Sift confectioners' sugar over top.

Makes 12 servings.

No-Bake Blackberry Cheesecake

1 ready-to-use graham cracker crust
1 3-ounce package blackberry gelatin
1 cup boiling water
2 8-ounce packages cream cheese, softened
1 cup milk
½ cup fresh blackberries, washed and picked over

Combine gelatin and boiling water in large mixer bowl; stir to dissolve gelatin. Add cream cheese and beat until smooth. Beat in milk. Pour into crust. Refrigerate until set. Garnish with fresh blackberries. Makes 8 to 10 servings.

You can sweeten berries with granulated or maple sugar or light syrup. A touch of balsamic vinegar along with the maple sweetener adds a nice flavor.

Easy Blackberry Torte

1 package yellow cake mix
1 8-ounce container frozen whipped topping, thawed
1 24-ounce jar blackberry cobbler filling

Heat oven to 350 degrees. Spray two 9- by 1½-inch round layer pans with non-stick cooking spray.

Prepare, bake and cool cake according to package directions. Chill cooled layers for ease in splitting. Split each cake layer into 2 thin layers. Place first cake layer on serving plate and spread with ⅓ of whipped topping. Put second cake layer in place and spread with one-half of cobbler filling. Put third cake layer in place and spread with one-half of remaining whipped topping. Top with fourth cake layer, spoon remaining topping around edge and spread remaining filling in center. Chill at least 1 hour before serving. Makes 12 servings.

Blackberry Pretzel Salad

2 cups pretzels, crushed
⅓ cup sugar
¾ cup melted margarine
8 ounces cream cheese, softened
1 cup sugar
1 12-ounce container frozen whipped topping, thawed
2 3-ounce packages raspberry gelatin
2 ½ cups boiling water
1 cup frozen blackberries, thawed

Mix pretzels, ⅓ cup sugar and melted margarine and press into a 9- by 13-inch pan. Bake at 350 degrees about 8 minutes. Cream the cream cheese and add 1 cup sugar and whipped topping. Mix and spread over cooled crust. Combine gelatin and boiling water and blackberries. Chill. When slightly set, pour over creamed mixture and crust. Refrigerate. Serves 10.

Blackberry Muffins

2 cups self-rising flour, divided
2 cups fresh blackberries, washed and picked over
1/4 cup sugar plus 2 tablespoons
1 egg
1 cup milk
1/4 cup butter or margarine, melted

Heat oven to 400 degrees. Combine 1/4 cup of the flour with fresh blackberries. Set aside. Mix together 1 3/4 cups self-rising flour and sugar. Combine with egg, milk and melted butter. Add blackberries. Bake in greased muffin pans for about 20 minutes. Makes 1 dozen.

Cook berries only lightly, because the delicate fruit will turn to mush otherwise.

Louie's Blackberry Consommé

1 ½ quarts blackberries, washed and picked over
2 cups sugar
2 tablespoons flour
3 cups water
½ cup sour cream
½ cup whipping cream
½ cup blackberry wine

Simmer blackberries in water for 10 minutes. Force the mixture through a sieve or puree in a blender.

Combine sugar and flour. Stir in water, sour cream, whipping cream and blackberry wine. Add the mixture to the pureed berries.

Slowly bring the soup to a boil, stirring constantly. Boil 2 minutes, then let cool. Chill and serve, garnishing each portion with a few blackberries and a spoonful of sour cream.

If you would like to save soup for a later date, pour half of the soup into a freezer container and freeze. Remove the frozen block from the container, wrap in freezer-weight foil and store. To serve frozen portion, defrost at room temperature and serve. Makes 6 servings.

Blackberry Crumble

1 24-ounce jar blackberry cobbler filling
¾ cup self-rising flour
⅓ cup sugar
½ stick margarine

Pour cobbler filling into 9- by 13-inch baking dish. Combine flour, sugar and margarine and mix until crumbled. Sprinkle over cobbler mix. Bake in a 350-degree oven for 35 to 40 minutes or until brown.

Makes 8 servings.

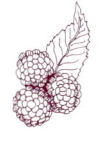

The blackberry is the scarcest of all American berries.

Blackberry Salad

1 tablespoon Dijon mustard
1/3 cup blackberry vinegar (see page 15)
1 teaspoon salt
1 teaspoon freshly ground black pepper
1 cup light olive oil
1 bunch red leaf lettuce, washed and dried
1 pint fresh blackberries, washed and picked over

Beat mustard, vinegar, salt and pepper together, then add oil slowly until the dressing is emulsified. Toss lettuce with 1/3 cup dressing and top with blackberries. Serve at once. Makes 4 servings.

Blackberry-Basil Marinade

1/3 cup blackberry vinegar (see page 15)
1/3 cup vegetable oil
2 tablespoons chopped fresh basil leaves
1/3 teaspoon salt
1/3 teaspoon freshly ground black pepper

Whisk together vinegar, oil, basil, salt and black pepper. Use to marinate vegetables.

Blackberry Vinaigrette

1/3 cup blackberry vinegar (see page 15)
1/4 cup honey
1/4 cup olive oil
2 tablespoons lemon juice
1 1/2 teaspoons dry mustard
Salt and pepper to taste

Combine all ingredients and mix thoroughly. Makes 1 1/4 cups. Serve over vegetable salad or favorite fruit.

Blackberry Mustard

Combine 1/4 cup blackberry jam with 1 cup prepared yellow mustard. Use as a dip for summer sausage or cheese or as a sandwich spread.

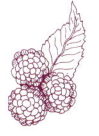

A pint of berries serves 2 to 4 people.

Old-Fashioned Blackberry Jam Pudding

4 eggs
1 ½ cups all-purpose flour
1 cup sugar
1 teaspoon cinnamon
½ teaspoon nutmeg
1 teaspoon baking powder
1 cup milk
1 cup blackberry jam

Beat eggs until light. Combine flour, sugar, cinnamon, nutmeg and baking powder. Add milk and jam. Mix well. Pour into 9- by 13-inch pan and bake at 350 degrees for 30 to 40 minutes. Serve warm with ice cream. Serves 6.

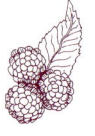

Cultivation of the blackberry began around 1825.

Quick Blackberry Tarts

1 package frozen tart shells
1 24-ounce jar blackberry cobbler filling

Place tart shells on cookie sheet. Fill with cobbler filling and bake according to package directions until crust is golden brown. Garnish with whipped cream. Makes 6 servings.

Berries and Pudding

1 package frozen puff pastry, thawed
1 8-ounce package lemon pudding
Macaroon cookies
½ cup fresh blackberries

Roll out the dough and bake according to package directions. Prepare pudding according to package directions. Spoon pudding to edges of pastry.

Scatter with fresh blackberries. Crumble macaroons and sprinkle over dessert. Makes 6 servings.

The best way to enjoy blackberries is plain for breakfast or with a splash of whipped cream for dessert.

Blackberry Angel Cake

½ cup sugar
1 tablespoon cornstarch
1 ½ cups frozen blackberries, thawed and drained; reserve syrup
1 prepared angel food cake

Combine sugar and cornstarch in small saucepan; stir in blackberry syrup. Cook and stir over medium heat until mixture comes to a boil. Remove from heat; add blackberries. Cool slightly, then pour over top of cake and let run down sides. Topping will become firm as it cools. Makes 16 servings.

Blackberry Yogurt Breeze

3 cups blackberries, fresh or frozen
3 cups low-fat vanilla yogurt
6 tablespoons honey
2 ¼ cups milk
½ cup whole blackberries

Puree blackberries in a blender. Add yogurt and honey and puree about 30 seconds, until smooth and thickened. With the motor running, add the milk and process for 30 to 40 seconds, until thick. Serve immediately, garnished with whole berries.

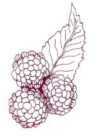

A cup of blackberries contains about 75 calories.

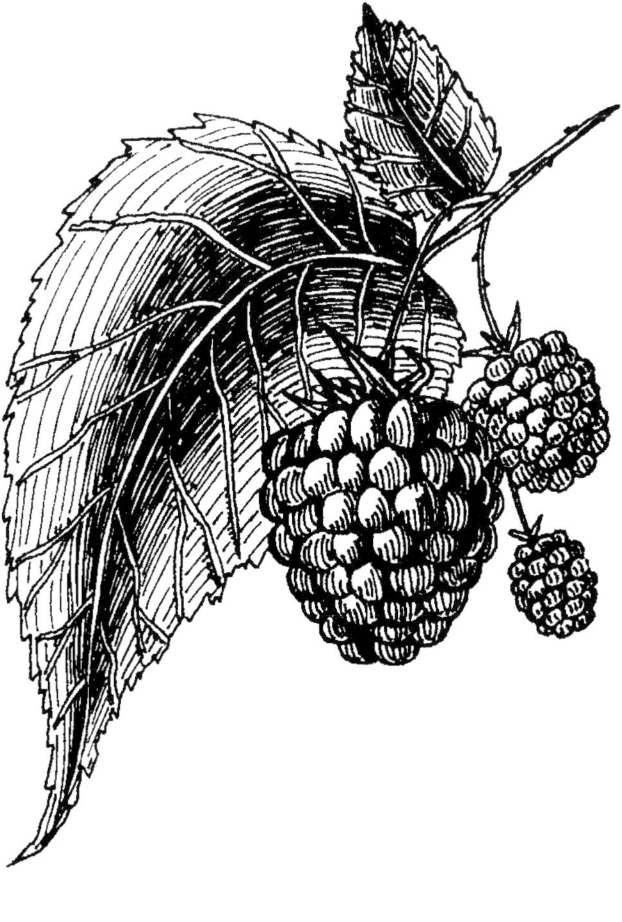

Blackberries and Summer Fruits

1 small firm-ripe cantaloupe, cut in 1/2-inch wedges
1 nectarine, halved, pitted and cut in wedges
3 kiwis, peeled and sliced
2 plums, pitted, halved or quartered
1 cup small watermelon balls
1/4 pound Champagne grapes
1 cup strawberries
1/2 cup blackberries
Lemon sherbet

Arrange cantaloupe wedges to fill bottom of serving platter. Top with nectarine, kiwis, plums, watermelon, grapes, strawberries and blackberries. Cover and chill until serving time. Garnish with large scoop of lemon sherbet. Makes 4 to 6 servings.

The peak season is in June and July, but blackberries are readily available in May and August and there is also a fall crop.

Easy Blackberry-Banana Bread

$3/4$ cup sugar
$1/2$ cup margarine
2 eggs
2 bananas, mashed
1 $1/2$ cups blackberries, frozen or thawed
2 cups flour
1 $1/2$ teaspoons baking powder
$1/2$ teaspoon baking soda
$1/2$ cup pecans, chopped

Cream sugar and margarine. Add eggs, one at a time, and mix well. Add bananas and blackberries. Mix remaining ingredients and add to blackberry mixture. Pour into a greased loaf pan. Bake at 350 degrees for 1 hour. May be served hot or cold. Makes 1 loaf.

Custard and Berries

1 4-ounce package French vanilla instant pudding mix
½ cup sugar
1 teaspoon vanilla
4 cups milk
1 8-ounce container frozen whipped topping, thawed
1 package puff pastry shells
1 cup fresh blackberries, washed and picked over

Combine pudding mix, sugar and vanilla with milk. Stir until smooth. Fold in whipped topping and chill under cold. Prepare pastry shells according to package directions. Fill with custard and top with fresh blackberries.

Blackberry Butter

1 stick butter
2 cups fresh blackberries or 1 pound frozen and thawed,
  pureed and seeded
1 cup sugar

Melt the butter and stir in blackberries and sugar. Remove from heat and stir until sugar is dissolved. Store in refrigerator for up to 2 weeks. When ready to serve, warm and drizzle over pancakes or French toast or hot biscuits. Makes 2 cups.

Blackberry Sorbet

2 cups sugar
2 cups water
4 cups fresh blackberries, washed and picked over
2 to 3 tablespoons fresh lemon juice
2 tablespoons black currant syrup

Stir sugar and water together in a 2½-quart souffle dish. Cook, uncovered, at 100 percent in a high-power microwave oven for 3 minutes. Stir thoroughly, being sure there are no grains on the bottom of the dish. Cover with a lid or microwave plastic wrap. Cook for 6 minutes. Prick plastic, if used, to release steam. Remove from oven and uncover. Let cool. Refrigerate several hours or overnight.

Press blackberries through a sieve. Whisk in lemon juice, black currant syrup and sugar syrup. Refrigerate until cold. Place in an ice-cream machine and freeze according to manufacturer's instructions. Makes 10 servings.

Note: Low-power variation: Cook uncovered 5 minutes; covered, 11 minutes.

To seed blackberries, run them through a food mill or puree in a food processor and push the crushed berries through a sieve.

Hartsfield Family Blackberry Jam Cake

2 cups brown sugar
1½ cups shortening
6 eggs
4 cups flour
1 teaspoon allspice
1 teaspoon each cinnamon, nutmeg and soda
1 tablespoon black pepper
1 cup buttermilk
2 cups blackberry jam
1 pound raisins
1 pound currants

Cream brown sugar and shortening together in large mixing bowl. Add eggs, one at a time. Sift together flour, allspice, cinnamon, nutmeg, soda and black pepper. Add to creamed mixture alternately with buttermilk and jam. Add raisins and currants. Pour into a greased and floured tube pan. Bake at 325 degrees for 1 hour or until a toothpick inserted in center comes out clean.

Berry-Cherry Pie

2 9-inch ready-to-bake pie crusts
2 tablespoons quick-cooking tapioca
¾ cup sugar
¼ teaspoon salt
3 cups fresh blackberries, washed and picked over
3 cups pitted sweet cherries
2 tablespoons butter

Heat oven to 425 degrees. Line pie pan with bottom crust.

Stir together tapioca, sugar and salt in large mixing bowl. Add blackberries and cherries and toss to mix well. Pour berry mixture into crust. Dot with bits of butter. Cover with the top crust. Flute edges and cut a vent in top crust. Bake for 25 minutes and reduce heat to 350 degrees and bake until crust is browned, about 35 minutes.

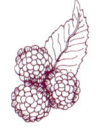

When North America was originally settled there were few blackberry brambles because of the heavy forests. Blackberries spread as the land was cleared.

Kentucky Jam Cake

1 cup raisins
½ cup Kentucky bourbon
½ cup unseasoned bread crumbs
1½ cups unsalted butter
2 cups sugar
6 eggs
3 cups all-purpose flour
1 teaspoon baking soda
1½ teaspoons cinnamon
1¼ teaspoons cloves
1¼ teaspoons allspice
2 tablespoons unsweetened cocoa
¾ cup buttermilk
1 tablespoon vanilla
2 cups blackberry jam
½ cup walnuts, coarsely chopped and toasted

Soak raisins in bourbon for 30 minutes. Heat oven to 325 degrees.

Spray a 10-inch Bundt pan with non-stick cooking spray and coat with bread crumbs.

Cream butter and sugar in large mixing bowl until light and fluffy. Add eggs, one at a time, beating well after each addition. Sift together flour, baking soda, spices and cocoa. Set aside.

Combine buttermilk and vanilla. Fold flour mixture into sugar mixture, alternating with the buttermilk mixture. Do not beat.

Drain raisins and fold into batter along with the jam and walnuts. Pour into prepared pan and bake for 60 to 70 minutes. Cool and unmold onto a cake rack.

To make icing: Melt ½ cup butter in a saucepan over medium heat. Add 1 cup brown sugar and stir for 2 minutes. Slowly add ¼ cup milk and bring to a boil. Remove from heat and stir in 1 tablespoon vanilla and 2½ cups confectioners' sugar. Beat until creamy and smooth. Thin with a little bourbon. Drizzle over warm cake. Makes 12 servings.

ACKNOWLEDGMENTS

Mary Frentz
Virginia Crump
The Lexington Herald-Leader Co.
Louie and Ruby Emmons
Bob Snider
Bob Slone

Special thanks to:
Cliff Shumate
Don Hammonds
Marshall Fryman
and all the personnel
at WindStone Farms

INDEX

Basil Marinade, Blackberry 46
Berried Treasure 18
Breads
  Easy Blackberry-Banana Bread 55
  Blackberry Tea Bread 26
Butter, Blackberry 56
Cakes
  Aunt Gin's Jam Cake 6
  Bourbon Jam Cake 7
  Blackberry Bundt Cake 16
  Blackberry Cake 36
  Blackberry Dump Cake 34
  Hartsfield Family Jam Cake 58
  Hidden Berry Cake 39
  Kentucky Jam Cake 60
  Rolling Blackberry Cake 35
  Blackberry Angel Cake 51
  Simple Jam Cake 33
  Crunch Cake, Blackberry 38
Cheesecakes
  Blackberry Cheesecake Bars 20
  No Bake Blackberry Cheesecake 40
  Blackberry Swirl Cheesecake 14
  Berry Good Cheesecake Bars 23
Cheese Fluff, Blackberry 19
Cobblers
  Margaret's Blackberry Cobbler 8
  Grandma's Blackberry Cobbler 30
Crumble, Blackberry 45
Drinks
  Triple Berry Refresher 27
  Blackberry Yogurt Breeze 52

Dumplings, Blackberry 25
  Louie's Blackberry Consommé 44
Muffins and Coffeecakes
  Berry Cream Coffee Cake 22
  Blackberry Muffins 43
Mousse, Blackberry 11
Mustard, Blackberry 47
Pies, Tarts and Tortes
  Berry-Cherry Pie 59
  Mountain Pie, Blackberry 9
  Blackberry Pie 29
  Easy Blackberry Torte 41
  Quick Blackberry Tarts 49
Puddings and Custards
  Luscious Blackberry Custard 31
  Pudding, Old-Fashioned Jam 48
  Triple Layer Pudding 13
  Berries and Pudding 50
  Custard and Berries 56
Puree, Blackberry 16
Salads
  Black and Blue Salad 24
  Grilled Chicken Salad 10
  Blackberry Pretzel Salad 42
  Blackberry Salad 46
  Blackberries and Summer Fruits 54
Sherbets and Sorbets
  Blackberry Sherbet 32
  Blackberry Sorbet 57
Vinaigrette, Blackberry 47
Vinegar, Blackberry 15